THE LOST BOYS

by Pastor Jake Bishop

Climbing Angel Publishing

THE LOST BOYS
Written by Pastor Jake Bishop

Transcribed by Tonya Celeste Hobbs
Edited by Lisa Soland
Text copyright © 2023 Jake Bishop

Published in 2023 by:
Climbing Angel Publishing
PO Box 32381
Knoxville, Tennessee 37930
http://www.ClimbingAngel.com

First Edition: June 2023
Printed in the United States of America

Cover painting: "The Return of the Prodigal Son"
    by Rembrandt.
Graphic Design: Climbing Angel Publishing

ISBN: 978-1-956218-27-5
Library of Congress Control Number: 2023908211

This book is dedicated to my two boys,
Knox and Haddon.

May I always point you to your true Father.

BULLSEYE

There are a lot of great stories about the Olympics, but the one I think about the most doesn't involve Michael Phelps, Simone Biles, or any of the other usual suspects. It's a story about an athlete named Matthew Emmons, a sharpshooter who dreamed of representing the United States. He achieved that goal in 2004 and went to Athens as a favorite to win gold. All of his training, his entire life, had led to that moment, but if he were nervous, you never would have known it. On the biggest stage, Matthew was having the event of his life.

As a sport, sharpshooting isn't too hard to explain. To put it simply, you have a gun and a target, and you try to hit bullseyes. And that's what Matthew was doing that day. So much so that going into the final shot, if he hit another bullseye, he would return to the United States with the gold medal.

This next shot was the biggest of his life. Everything was riding on this next moment. So, here's Matthew Emmons, 23 years old;

he's been working for this his whole life. He finds the target in his sight, takes a deep breath, and shoots. With ice in his veins, he nails it—a perfect bullseye—exactly where he aimed! Then he looks for his name on the scoreboard and discovers he has come in eighth place. Matthew shot a bullseye and came in eighth place! He executed a perfect shot, exactly where he was aiming, but here's the problem. *Matthew focused on the wrong target*. He was aiming at the target next to his.

This story illustrates an important point. As Christians, we know what the target is. It's Jesus. To abide in Him. To become more like Him. And to do the things He did. But it's surprisingly easy to get off target and not know it. And we're going to see in our passage that there are actually two ways to miss the mark.

THE TWO GROUPS

We will be studying Luke 15:11-32, but to understand the context of Jesus' story, we will begin with verses 1 and 2.

> *Now the tax collectors and sinners were all drawing near to hear him. And the Pharisees and the scribes grumbled, saying, "This man receives sinners and eats with them."*
> (Luke 15:1-2)

Luke tells us that there are two groups listening to Jesus. There are the tax collectors and sinners, and then there are the Pharisees and scribes. So, who are these people? The tax collectors and sinners were the moral outcasts. They were the ones who had utterly done away with the morality of their childhoods. They were the rebels looking for self-fulfillment. They were the ones who had seemingly abandoned God. But they were also the ones who were drawn to Jesus. Throughout the Gospels, they see something in Jesus that draws them to Him, like a moth to a flame.

Then there are the Pharisees and scribes, who are just the opposite. They are the religious leaders who have held to the traditional morality of their upbringing. They are the ones who know the scriptures inside and out and worship God faithfully. These two groups are the polar opposites of each other.

The sinners and the tax collectors would have been looked down upon by everyone as dirty and unclean. The Pharisees would have been looked up to as the epitome of goodness. The word Pharisee literally means "the one who is separated." They are separated from everyone by their faithfulness to God's law. As you can imagine, the dynamic between the two groups is pretty awkward. The good guys (the Pharisees and scribes) look down upon these bad guys (the tax collectors and sinners). And

they can't believe that Jesus would have anything to do with them.

So, Jesus is placed smack dab in the middle of this awkward social dynamic. What's He going to say? How's He going to respond?

Well, Jesus answers the way He often does—by telling stories. Here, He shares three. The first story is a shorter one about a sheep that gets lost, and a shepherd who leaves the 99 to find it. Then He tells a similar story about a woman who loses a coin and then tears her house upside down to locate it. Finally, Jesus tells a third story, the most famous one. The story is almost cliché at this point because we hear it so often. Whether you are part of a church community or not, this well-known story has become a part of our cultural vocabulary. We call it the *Parable of the Prodigal Son*. But, as we work through these verses, we will find that this is not just a story about one son. There are two brothers, and they represent Jesus' two sets of listeners. The younger brother represents the tax collectors and the sinners, and the older brother represents the religious leaders of the day.

To reflect this, Jesus tells the parable in two acts. In verses 11-24 He talks about the younger brother, and in verses 25-32 He talks

about the older brother. So, let's start by focusing on Act One.

And he said, "There was a man who had two sons. And the younger of them said to his father, 'Father, give me the share of property that is coming to me.' And he divided his property between them.
(Luke 15:11-12)

THE YOUNGER BROTHER

So, a man has two sons—a younger one and an older one. The younger son comes to his father with a strange request. He says to him, "Give me my inheritance." This young man was right to expect an inheritance, but there were rules about this sort of thing. If the father had two sons, the older son would get two-thirds of everything, and the younger son would inherit one-third. So this younger son is right to understand that he is getting one-third of what his father has.

But as we know, an inheritance comes *after* the father is dead, not *before*. But this younger son approaches his father and says, "I'm not waiting for you to die. Give me my inheritance now." The younger son is basically saying to his dad, "You are dead to me." This is a son spitting in his father's face, saying, "I don't want you. I just want your stuff." And,

that's painful when a parent thinks about one of their kids saying this to them. But it's even more tragic when we remember who the father represents in this story. The older son represents the Pharisees and scribes, the younger brother represents the tax collectors and sinners, but the father represents God. So this is a picture of a complete rejection of God. It is as if someone is saying to God, "I don't want you; I just want your stuff." It is a shocking request.

Not many days later, the younger son gathered all he had and took a journey into a far country, and there he squandered his property in reckless living. And when he had spent everything, a severe famine arose in that country, and he began to be in need. So he went and hired himself out to one of the citizens of that country, who sent him into his fields to feed pigs. And he was longing to be fed with the pods that the pigs ate, and no one gave him anything. "But when he came to himself, he said, 'How many of my father's hired servants have more than enough bread, but I perish here with hunger! I will arise and go to my father, and I will say to him, "Father, I have sinned against heaven and before you. I am no longer worthy to be called your son. Treat me as one of your hired servants."'
(Luke 15:13-19)

The younger son takes his inheritance, heads to a distant country, and completely blows it all. He squanders it. And that is why we call him the *prodigal* son. We have heard this story so often that we may think *prodigal* means wayward, but it doesn't. The actual definition of *prodigal* is to be wastefully extravagant. Verse 13 tells us that the son "squandered his property in reckless living." That is what makes him a prodigal. He goes off and is recklessly extravagant. He spends all of his father's inheritance, and the boy's life begins to spiral out of control.

Just when he thinks things can't get any worse, a famine comes. The economy turns upside down, and he has to get a job working with pigs, an unclean animal to Jesus' Jewish audience. This guy has truly hit rock-bottom.

He's left with one option: there's nowhere to go but home. There's no way he can be a son again, of course. That ship has clearly sailed. But maybe he could be a servant. He doesn't expect the father to forgive him. How could he? But maybe, just maybe, he will at least give him a job. At least it would get him out of the pigsty.

And he arose and came to his father. But while he was still a long way off, his father saw him and felt compassion, and ran and embraced him and kissed him.
(Luke 15:20)

This story has become so familiar for many of us that we can miss how extraordinary this moment is, but I beg you not to do that. Slow down. Read verse 20 again, and then reread it. Meditate on it. All that this son has put his father through, but here we have a father still watching for his son. He has been standing on the porch, day after day, hoping to see him walk into town. The son had wished his father dead. He humiliated him. He took all of his stuff and ran off. But, through it all, the father had not stopped loving him. He had not given up on him. And when the father sees him, he can't help but run to him and meet him with extravagant love!

Let me ask, how do you picture God's heart toward you? I'm not just looking for a good theological answer. As you read through this book, I am asking you how you imagine God feels about you? Let me take it a step further. Picture yourself at rock-bottom. Maybe you are there right now. When you're in the metaphorical pigsty of your own making, how do you think God feels about you? Do you picture God as this father in our story? Showing compassion and then running to you with his arms open wide, embracing you with a fatherly kiss? Because that's the image Jesus is creating for us. That is what Jesus is teaching us. Jesus says, "You've

rebelled, you've wished God dead, you've done things your own way, and you think all of your bridges have been burned. But God never stopped loving you!" The son didn't know it, but he was indescribably loved even while he was living with the pigs.

The same is true for each of us. Your sin does not cancel out God's love for you.

GOD NEVER STOPS LOVING YOU

If you feel you are at rock-bottom right now, remember that God loves to use *rock-bottom* to bring people back to Himself. And if you run to Him, the Father stands ready to take you back into His loving arms. We can picture the son saying to himself on the walk home, "I gotta get the words right. I need to make the speech perfect. It's the only way to convince my dad to welcome me back." But notice, the father won't even hear of it.

And the son said to him, 'Father, I have sinned against heaven and before you. I am no longer worthy to be called your son.' But the father said to his servants, 'Bring quickly the best robe, and put it on him, and put a ring on his hand, and shoes on his feet. And bring the fattened calf and kill it, and let us eat and celebrate. For this my son was dead, and is

alive again; he was lost, and is found.' And
they began to celebrate.
(Luke 15:21-24)

This kid shows up, ashamed, in dirty rags, and the father brings the best robe and welcomes him back into the family. Jesus wants to show us that our God is rich in mercy.

In his book, *Gentle and Lowly*, Dane Ortlund reminds us:

> *"That God is rich in mercy means that your regions of deepest shame and regret are not hotels through which divine mercy passes but homes in which divine mercy abides. It means the things about you that make you cringe most, make him hug hardest. It means his mercy is not calculating and cautious, like ours. It is unrestrained, flood-like, sweeping, magnanimous. It means our haunting shame is not a problem for him, but the very thing he loves most to work with. It means our sins do not cause his love to take a hit. Our sins cause his love to surge forward all the more. It means on that day when we stand before him, quietly, unhurriedly, we will weep with relief, shocked at how impoverished a view of his mercy-rich heart we had."*

The father responds with mercy. And not only that, he throws his son an awesome party. He kills the fattened calf, and they all eat, drink, and celebrate because the son has returned.

The whole town is celebrating because the lost son is home. It's an absolutely beautiful story. But one person is missing from the party.

THE OLDER BROTHER

"Now his older son was in the field, and as he came and drew near to the house, he heard music and dancing. And he called one of the servants and asked what these things meant. And he said to him, 'Your brother has come, and your father has killed the fattened calf, because he has received him back safe and sound.' But he was angry and refused to go in. His father came out and entreated him, but he answered his father, 'Look, these many years I have served you, and I never disobeyed your command, yet you never gave me a young goat, that I might celebrate with my friends. But when this son of yours came, who has devoured your property with prostitutes, you killed the fattened calf for him!' And he said to him, 'Son, you are always with me, and all that is mine is yours. It was fitting to celebrate and be glad, for this your brother was dead, and is alive; he was lost, and is found.'"
(Luke 15:25-32)

The artist, Rembrandt van Rijn, shares his take on the story with one of his most famous paintings—*The Return of the Prodigal Son*, c. 1661–1669. The publisher used it for the cover of this book.

When I see this painting, my eyes go straight to the younger son and his father. It's a beautiful picture of repentance and grace. The Father's "mercy-rich heart" is on full display. But you'll notice off to the right, there's another guy, and he doesn't look so happy. He's not celebrating at all. And here's what's interesting—that's the older brother. Rembrandt took some creative license with this work of art because the older brother wasn't actually there when the younger brother returned home, but he makes an important point. Our eyes go straight to the prodigal and his dad. And rightfully so; it's beautiful and moving. But throughout the story, the older brother lurks in the background. The prodigal comes home, and we celebrate! The whole town celebrates! But I couldn't help but wonder, what did the older son think when his brother came home? Jesus doesn't give us that information, but, using my imagination, I think the older brother might say something like this if you asked him what he was feeling:

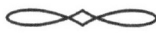

"I have never been angrier than I am right now. He's home. And not only that, my father has welcomed him with open arms. It's like my father doesn't even remember what my younger brother put him

through. But I haven't forgotten. Asking for his inheritance early. Abandoning us. Blowing Dad's money on prostitutes. It just goes to show that he only thinks about himself. That's all he's ever thought about—himself. I mean, if you could've seen my poor father, day after day, standing on the porch waiting for him. That poor old man would not give up. I told him every day, 'Dad, give up. He's not coming back,' but I guess I was wrong. I didn't think he'd have the guts to come back, but he's here.

"And you know, I wish I had seen him first. Since he left, I've been thinking about what I would say to him, and I know exactly what I'd do. I would've looked him straight in the face, and I would've told him the truth. That there's no place for him in our family. He doesn't even deserve to be in the same room as our dad. He doesn't deserve it! But unfortunately, I didn't see him first. I was doing what I always do. I was working. I was doing what honorable men do. And then I came in, and I heard the music. And I asked one of the servants, 'What's going on?' but I already knew. He was back. And Dad saw him first.

"Call me crazy, but people should get what they deserve. I've worked hard for my father every single day, and I've never disobeyed him. He owes me. But how many parties has he thrown for me? Zero. I deserve a fattened calf every day, but he wouldn't even give me a goat. And yet, for this pathetic excuse for a son, he does this. So I refused to go to the party. I wasn't going to give him or my father the

satisfaction. I want to make sure they know my position on the whole thing. And my position is that I'm angry! I don't think it's right. I was so mad I could feel my fist balling up. I was so angry; I just wanted to scream. I can't even put into words how angry I was and still am. And then my dad came and found me. He left the party to come find me. And let me tell you, when I saw him, I didn't hold back. I let him know what I was thinking. I let him know that it was unfair; I told him I deserved better. I reminded him of all the things that I had done for him, and I totally unloaded everything that I was feeling. I fully expected him to respond the same way. He's always been slow to anger. But the way I disrespected him, how could he not?

"But here's something I can't stop thinking about. When I looked into my father's eyes, I didn't see anger. I saw love. He looked at me and said something in a soft voice. I can't remember what it was. I was too mad to listen. But he pleaded with me to come in, and then he went back into the party. The party is still going on. It's been going on for a few days. I'm still outside. And honestly, I don't know what I'm going to do."

So, one story, two very different perspectives. A father who celebrates and an older brother who can't help but be bitter. To understand Jesus' point, we need to go back to

the very beginning—the context of Luke 15:2. Who is Jesus telling this parable to? He's responding to the grumbling of the Pharisees and scribes. That is who the story is primarily for—the *older brothers* in the crowd. And that's why Jesus ends the story the way He does. It doesn't end well. This parable doesn't have a happy ending. Instead, it ends on a cliffhanger. The older brother has to decide whether he's going to join the party or not.

It's crazy how the story starts—the bad guy who ran off with all the money is "*inside*" the party. He's no longer alienated from his father. He's back in a relationship with him. But the good boy is "*outside*" the party. He's alienated from God. Jesus is challenging us to do something radical. He wants us to rethink sin. We must rethink what it means to be lost and alienated from God.

When I was in college, God used this parable to completely change the direction of my life. Growing up, I knew the gospel. It was preached to me often. I also understood that I was a sinner. But here's what I did not understand. I knew I was a sinner, but I didn't think I was that bad. In my mind, many other people were a lot worse sinners than me. So, I would read this story or hear it preached, and I would look around the room and say, "I hope these people hear it because there are a lot of prodigals in this room who need to come

home." And let me admit; my heart was often cold to God.

Some of you have read this book up to this point and are wondering how this story relates to *you*. My life was changed when I was given the book, *The Prodigal God* by Timothy Keller. God used this book, a beautiful exposition of this parable, to help me truly understand the gospel. I can't overstate the effect it has had on my life. In the book, Keller shows how Jesus is doing something radical in this parable. He is redefining sin and repentance, and all of us "older brothers" would be wise to pay attention.

In Act One, the younger brother's story, we get an obvious illustration of sin. We read that story and see a man dishonoring his father, sleeping with prostitutes, and seeking self-fulfillment at all costs. We look at that and say, "That's sin." But in Act Two, Jesus turns the tables because we discover that *both sons are lost*. Both sons are alienated from the father. Going back to the original illustration about the Olympian, it turns out that both sons are missing the target. But here's the dangerous thing—*the older brother doesn't know it*. The older brother thinks he's hitting the bullseye, but, in actuality, he will come in eighth place.

Both brothers have used the father to get what they want. One did it by being really bad,

and the other did it by being really good. The younger son is obvious about it. He walks up to the father and says, "You're dead to me; give me my inheritance. I only want you for your stuff." But the older brother did precisely the same thing. He rejected the father too, but he did it by being good. He followed his father's rules but never actually *wanted* the father. He just wanted his stuff.

This is so important. Jesus' parable shows us that there are two ways to be your own Lord and Savior. You can be the younger brother and make life all about self-fulfillment and getting what you want. But, you can also reject Jesus through self-righteousness—by doing all the *right things* so that you feel that you don't need Him.

If you are an "older brother," you obey, you do what God asks, but you don't do it out of love for God. You do it to use Him. You do it to put Him in your debt. All your obedience is to get what you really want, *but it isn't God.*

Charles Haddon Spurgeon said, "The greatest enemy to human souls is the self-righteous spirit which makes men look to themselves for salvation." This is dangerous because you can check all the religious boxes but still be rejecting God. Jesus is telling this parable for *us*—church people. It is a warning for us to rethink sin. But we also need to rethink repentance.

When we think of repentance, we often think of just one side of it. We think of repentance as what the younger brother did. He goes off, makes mistakes, returns to the father, and brings his list. He plans to say, "Here are all the things I've done wrong. Forgive me." We go to God, and we get out our list. We say, "God, I'm sorry I gossiped, I'm sorry I was impatient, I'm sorry for that sexual sin in which I am entangled. I'm sorry."

And that absolutely is repentance, but this parable shows us that it has to go deeper than that. Remember, in this story, the older brother is outside the party. The father comes to him, and the older brother says, "I have never disobeyed you." And the father doesn't disagree. This older brother seems to have nothing on his list. But here's what we miss. We must also repent for doing the right things with the wrong motivations. And that's why Jesus uses the older brother to represent the Pharisees.

I've heard it said, talking about the Pharisees, that the main barrier between them and God wasn't their sin. It was their damnable good works. They rejected God by doing good. They rejected God by trying to be their own savior and not thinking they needed Jesus. They needed to repent of doing good things with the wrong motivation. Is that where you are today?

The story of the *Prodigal Son* takes aim at everyone. No one escapes unscathed. But we still have one remaining question to ask. If everyone is lost, if rule breakers and rule followers are lost, how can we be found?

When Jesus tells this story, He knows He's about to die. And He also knows who is going to have Him killed—the older brothers. Yet, even so, He's oozing with love. He's saying to them, "Come in. You are welcome. The Father will welcome you with open arms."

THE INVITATION

This story is an invitation to everyone. Maybe you're the younger brother and down with the pigs right now. And that's why you're here, reading these words, to find hope. Perhaps you're the older brother and have been trying to be your own savior. And you've been attending church for decades, but you've been reliable and consistent in order to get God in your debt. The story makes it clear either way. You are "*outside*" the party. Is God inviting you in?

Remember, there are two stories that Jesus tells before this one. Both involve something being lost and someone going out to find it. A sheep gets lost, and a shepherd goes out to find it. A coin gets lost, and a woman goes to find it. But in our story of the

prodigal son, that doesn't happen. The son runs off, and no one goes looking for him. In *The Prodigal God*, Keller points out that Jesus' audience would have recognized something. This was the older brother's job. He was supposed to go and bring the younger son back, returning honor to his family. But in this story, no one goes to get the brother in the far country. No one.

But here is what Jesus is doing. He wants to show us something. He's holding up an example of a bad older brother to point us to the fact that we have a really good older brother. The Bible tells us that our older brother is telling this story. Jesus is our older brother, and He did His job. He came from heaven to earth, to the far country, to get us. And He lived the perfect life that we couldn't live. Then He died the death we deserve, on a criminal's cross. He is the good older brother who has come for us.

So, that leaves us with some invaluable, self-examining questions. Are you an older brother, a younger brother, or a mixture of the two? How are you rejecting God? What do you need to repent of? Perhaps it's a sexual sin, lying, cheating, or stealing "younger brother" sin. Or maybe you need to repent of "older brother" sin—doing the right thing with the wrong motivation, trying to earn God's love and control Him.

No matter your answer, Jesus took it all onto the cross. Whether you reject Him as an older or younger brother, He died for both alike so we can run freely to the Father. How amazing that we can run to the Father and celebrate our older brother who came to the far country to get us because we were hopeless without Him.

PRAYER

Dear Lord, thank you for the story of the Prodigal Son. You are the master storyteller. Thank you for the literary image of the Father who loves us so very much. I pray that You help me to believe that. We hear so much about Your love that it seems to lose its power, and that's a shame. I pray that You awaken in me a full awareness of Your love. How amazing it is that you love me like this. Thank you, God, for my "older brother," Jesus, who came to get me, lived the life I couldn't, and died the death I deserved. I pray for those in my family and circle of friends who do not know You. Please, bring them to Yourself. Lord, I love you, and thank you for your infinite love for me.

ABOUT CLIMBING ANGEL
PUBLISHING

Climbing Angel Publishing exists for the purpose of sharing stories of hope and encouragement, aiding in the gathering together of community, and supporting the process of betterment. The following books are available at ClimbingAngel.com and major bookstores.

ADULT BOOKS: (Romans 8:28-30)

In His Image by Sam Polson
(English, Romanian, & Mandarin)
By Faith by Sam Polson (English & Romanian)
My Birthday Gift to Jesus by Lisa Soland
Without Ceasing by Dr. Dennis Davidson
SonLight: Daily Light from the Pages of God's Word
by Sam Polson
Corona Victus: Conquering the Virus of Fear
by Sam Polson (English & Romanian)
Art Bushing: His Diary, Letters, & Photographs of WWII
by Art Bushing
Art & Dotty: His Diary, Their Letters & Photographs of
WWII by Art Bushing
Trimisul by Stan Johnson (Romanian)
Life Changing Prayer by Sam Polson
The Climbing Angel Christmas Treasury, variety of authors
J. Calvin Coolidge: Letters from the Korean War
by J. Calvin Coolidge
Stories from Kingman, AZ: The Heart of Historic Route 66
by Loren B. Wilson

Pathways: Ancient Paths from the Pages of the Old Testament by Sam Polson
Jesus is Alive! by Mike Sager
My Mother's Bible by Sam Polson
The Lost Boys by Jake Bishop

CHILDREN'S BOOKS: (Philippians 4:8)

The Christmas Tree Angel by Lisa Soland
The Unmade Moose by Lisa Soland
Thump by Lisa Soland
Somebunny To Love by Lisa Soland
(English & Mandarin)
The Truth About God's Rainbow by Lisa Soland
God's Promises by Lisa Soland
The Boy & The Bagel Necklace by Lisa Soland
God's Hands and Feet by Lisa Soland
I Like To Be Quiet by Joni Caldwell
Wheels Off! by Karlie Saumier
Ella's Trip of a Lifetime by Melanie Ewbank
Because You Are Mine by Gayle Childress Greene
Jeremy Plays the Blues by Amy Oden Simpson
Bad Hair Day by Jasmyne Simpkins
I Like To Read by Joni Caldwell
Trunks Up! by Karlie Saumier
Perusha's Paradise by Bette Reed Smith
Ruby and the Treasure Within by Tonya Celeste Hobbs
Abby, the Wonder Dog & her Warrior Princess
by Melanie Ewbank
The Christmas Coat by Lisa Soland

3

The Single Sermon Series

.

THE LOST BOYS